MAKING SHELTER

Neil Champion

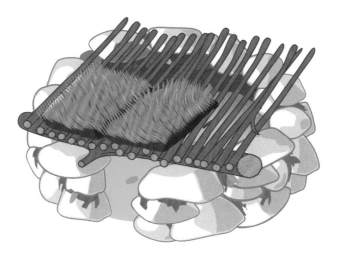

W

FRANKLIN WATTS

LONDON•SYDNEY

 An Appleseed Editions book

First published in 2010 by Franklin Watts
338 Euston Road, London NW1 3BH

Franklin Watts Australia
Hachette Children's Books
Level 17/207 Kent St, Sydney, NSW 2000

© 2010 Appleseed Editions

Created by Appleseed Editions Ltd,
Well House, Friars Hill, Guestling,
East Sussex TN35 4ET

Designed and illustrated by Guy Callaby
Edited by Stephanie Turnbull
Picture research by Su Alexander

ISBN 978 1 4451 0008 1

Dewey Classification: 613.6'9

A CIP catalogue for this book is available from the British Library.

Picture credits:
l = left, r = right, t = top, b = bottom
Contents page Ron Watts/Corbis; 4 PICIMPACT/Corbis; 5 Jason Friend/Alamy; 6 Jason
Spencer/Alamy; 7 Simon Belcher/Alamy; 8 Theo Allofs/Corbis; 10 Kevin Fleming/
Corbis; 11 Christian Kober/Robert Harding World Imagery/Corbis; 12 Steve Atkins
Photography/Alamy; 14 Dennis Cox/Alamy; 15 Neil Rabinowitz/Corbis; 16 Galen
Rowell/Corbis; 17 Paul A. Souders/Corbis; 18 Ron Watts/Corbis; 20 Rudy Sulgan/Corbis;
21 Peter Johnson/Corbis; 22 Janet Wishnetsky/Corbis; 23t Andre Jenny/Alamy, b Kim
Karpeles/Alamy; 24 John Warburton-Lee/Alamy; 25 Gunter Marx Photography/Corbis;
26 Hein van den Heuvel/Corbis; 27 John van Hasselt/Corbis Sygma; 28l Kevin Fleming/
Corbis, r Galen Rowell/Corbis; 29t Ron Watts/Corbis, b Neil Rabinowitz/Corbis

Front cover: Steve Atkins Photography/Alamy

Printed in China

Contents

Emergency homes

Imagine being stranded high on a mountain as night falls. The light is fading so quickly that you can't walk any further. It's getting colder, too. If you stay outside for much longer you will almost certainly get **frostbite**. Could you make a shelter for the night – and do it fast?

If you're climbing a mountain, you should start early and get back down to shelter well before evening. Storms often blow up in the afternoon.

Building skills

The ability to make a shelter is an important **bushcraft** skill. The key is knowing how to use materials you can find around you, such as branches, leaves or snow. A well-built shelter could mean the difference between a good night's sleep and a cold, uncomfortable night. It could even mean the difference between life and death.

▲ *You can use natural materials around you to make a shelter. Forests have plenty of branches, twigs, moss and leaves.*

All kinds of shelters

A shelter protects you from rain, snow, heat or cold. It keeps out wild animals and lets you rest, relax and recover your energy for the next day's adventures. A shelter can be a very simple construction that only lasts one night, or a more permanent design that will keep you safe and dry for weeks.

Keep it simple!

An emergency shelter is always going to be basic. Forget about comfort and concentrate on what you really need – a place to protect you from the weather and outside dangers. In this book you will learn how to turn simple materials into shelters that are suitable for all kinds of terrain and climates around the world.

TRUE SURVIVAL STORY

JAMIE NEALE was on a backpacking trip to Australia in 2009 when he got lost in dense bushland in the Blue Mountains, near Sydney. It was foggy, wet and cold and Jamie had no tools to build a proper shelter. Instead, he crawled into hollows under logs to sleep at night. It wasn't ideal, but it was good enough to keep him alive until he was rescued nearly two weeks later.

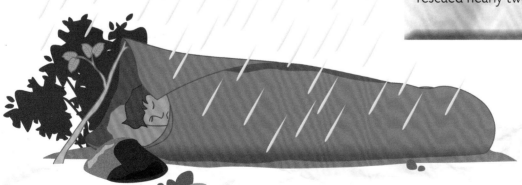

◄ *Even a very basic **tarpaulin** shelter can keep you covered and dry for the night.*

Natural shelters

Before you start building a shelter, have a good look around – there might be a ready-made natural shelter you can use instead. It might not be the most comfortable place, but it could save you a lot of time and energy. This could be especially useful if it's late in the evening.

Tree shelters

There are lots of natural shelters in forests. You might be able to crawl into a standing or fallen hollow tree. You could also lie in the shelter of a fallen tree that has a large spread of roots or branches. This will at least keep heavy rain off and protect you from the wind.

▼ *This hollow tree trunk could make an ideal emergency shelter for the night.*

Cave shelters

Caves can make great ready-made homes. For thousands of years, people have used caves as emergency shelters or even as permanent houses. Some caves, such as **howffs** in the Scottish Highlands, are small spaces beneath overhanging rocks. Other caves are made up of many underground rooms linked by winding passages. In these caves, always stay near the entrance so you don't get lost or injured inside.

DID YOU KNOW?
Animals like to shelter in caves, too. Make sure your cave is empty before you settle down for the night!

◀ *Caves are very useful shelters. They can protect you from wind, rain, snow or the hot desert sun.*

Ground cover

If you're in a hurry and can't see a cave or hollow tree, just look for large clumps of vegetation or piles of natural debris such as logs or leaves. You might be able to crawl behind or underneath them. If the ground is dry, find a hollow to curl up in. If you have time, pile leaves in it to lie on, and collect twigs or branches to rest over the top.

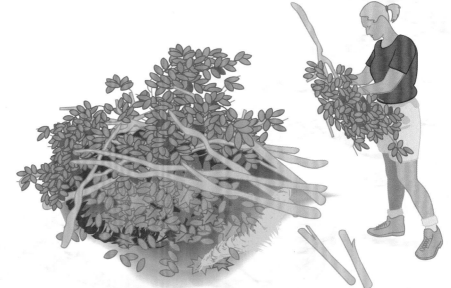

Choosing a site

When you're building a shelter, or even just putting up a tent, think carefully before you start work. Take a good look at the landscape and pick the best possible location. Here are some handy hints for deciding where to build.

Watch for water

It's a good idea to set up camp near water for cooking and washing, but don't get too close. If a river or stream floods in bad weather, your shelter could be damaged. Make sure the ground you're building on is dry and flat.

▶ This forest in Australia's Northern Territory floods during the rainy season. Any shelters built here would need to be on higher ground.

Stay sheltered

Find out which direction the wind is blowing from, and make sure the entrance to your shelter or tent is away from it. It's also a good idea to build near a natural barrier, such as a line of trees or raised ground, as this will help protect you from the wind.

Wind direction

Avoid hazards

Check that you're not building your shelter on top of an ant hill or other animal home. Try to avoid camping under trees, as dead branches may fall off in the wind. Don't make your shelter on uneven, stony ground that will be uncomfortable to lie on. Make sure your site isn't below a possible **landslide** or **avalanche**.

Don't go too low

Cold air sinks at night, which means that the lower an area of ground is, the chillier it will get. Low-lying areas such as valley bottoms are often called frost hollows. On clear, still nights, these areas trap so much cold air that frost can form. Stay warm by sticking to higher ground.

TRUE SURVIVAL STORY

MAURICE HERZOG led a mountaineering expedition in 1950 to climb Annapurna, in the Himalayas. On the way back, he and his team got lost in mist and had to camp for the night in a narrow **crevasse**. In the morning, they heard a strange hissing sound – and suddenly a huge avalanche of snow buried their shelter. Amazingly, they managed to dig through the snow and haul themselves out.

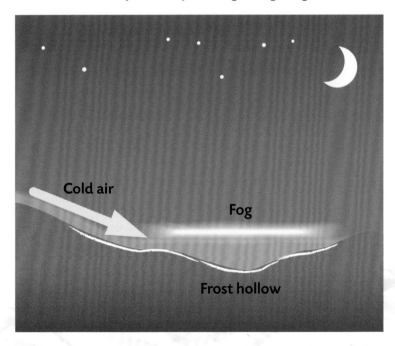

Cold air

Fog

Frost hollow

◀ *You can often spot a frost hollow because fog forms between the layer of cold air in the hollow and the warmer air above.*

Think smart!

Wherever you decide to build your shelter, make sure it's not too far from any natural materials you need, such as logs or leaves – otherwise you'll waste a lot of time and energy carrying them over to your site!

Building basics

When building a shelter, always use the best materials you can find, and choose a design that suits those materials. Make sure the shelter is strong enough to protect you from the weather. Also, remember that the effort you put into making it should reflect the length of your stay. If you're only staying one night, then it's a waste of time to construct something that will last a year.

Materials to use

Some of the best building materials in the wild are wood, **turf**, rocks, snow and leaves. You may also have useful materials with you, such as tarpaulin, a **poncho** or rope. Traditional **nomadic** people often use animal skins to build shelters, but these take a lot of time and skill to prepare.

▼ This nomad in Somalia is building a traditional **thatched**, wooden-framed hut called an aqal.

Different shapes

The shape of your shelter depends on the materials you can find to build with. For example, you can bend freshly-cut branches to make a tunnel or dome shape. Old, dead wood won't bend in the same way, so instead try making an 'A'-shaped frame. Snow is best made into a dome, called an **igloo**. Rocks can be piled up to make walls.

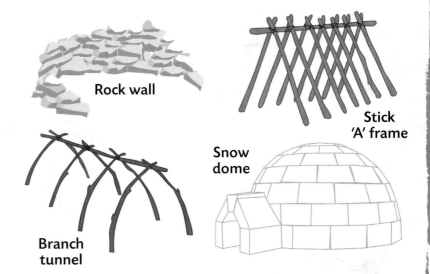

Rock wall

Stick 'A' frame

Snow dome

Branch tunnel

The perfect shape

Dome-shaped structures are the best shelters of all. The curved shape means that rain drains off and wind blows smoothly over the top. The curved blocks push inwards to hold the shape together, with no poles or walls that have to hold all the weight. You can learn how to build your own igloo on p18-19.

These domed shelters in Syria are called beehive houses. Large domes are ideal in hot places, as the curved shape forms a big, airy room.

Big or small?

You should also think about the size of your shelter. The bigger the shelter, the cooler it will be inside, so keep it small if the nights are going to be cold. You can plug gaps in the sides with mud or leaves to stop heat escaping. Remember to leave small ventilation holes, so air can get in and out.

Forest huts

Forests are full of ideal materials for building a warm, dry home for the night. All you need are branches, twigs and leaves – and the more you gather, the cosier your shelter will be. But don't get too carried away! You don't want night to fall before your hut is finished.

▲ *This shelter of branches has plenty of fallen leaves piled on top for **insulation**.*

Making a lean-to

A lean-to is a simple shelter made of branches that are propped up against something solid.

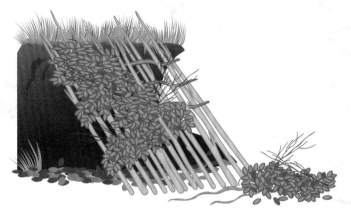

1. *Find ten or more straight branches about three metres (ten feet) long. Lean them against an earth bank or large tree. Make sure they create a space big enough to lie in.*

2. *Weave bendy twigs, fir branches, reeds or long grasses between the sticks, then fill the gaps with dead leaves and any other vegetation you can find. In winter, there might also be snow to add on top.*

A debris hut

You could also try making a debris hut. These use the same materials as a lean-to, but they stand alone.

1. *Dig a shallow trench just bigger than your body.*

2. *Line it with sticks and dry leaves.*

3. *Make a frame with two strong, forked branches and one long, thick branch.*

4. *Rest shorter branches on each side of the frame, then cover them with leaves and other vegetation.*

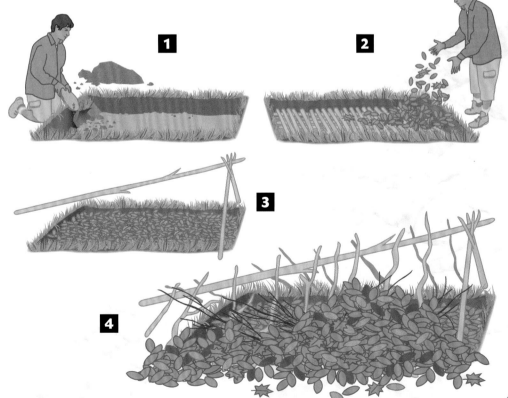

Jungle shelters

Jungles are rainy places, so you need to build a shelter with a good roof to keep you dry. Fortunately, jungles are also full of great natural building materials, such as huge palm leaves and long bamboo stems. However, you'll need a sharp knife to cut them.

Bamboo frames

Bamboo stems are long, straight poles that are perfect for building shelter frames. You could use them to make a lean-to (see page 13) or an 'A'-shaped frame. Look for long, thick vines to lash the poles together.

▶ *Bamboo stems, like those growing here, are very strong and are often used as a building material.*

Making a palm roof

To make a good roof for your shelter, you will need several large palm leaves.

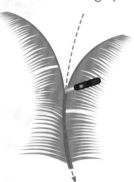

First, split each leaf in half lengthwise. Start from the tip or else they may break. Be very careful when using a knife.

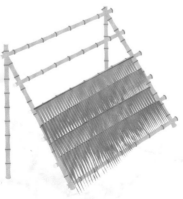

Next, layer the leaves across the frame, with the long fronds hanging down. Start at the bottom of the frame and work upwards.

Raised shelters

Heavy rain in the jungle can cause floods and leave the ground damp for a long time, so it's a good idea to make a raised platform of branches to sleep on. As well as keeping you dry, this will also protect you from insects and snakes!

▶ *These wooden houses in the Cameron Highlands, Malaysia, are built on stilts so they don't get flooded.*

Handy hammocks

Many jungle explorers carry **hammocks** to use as a quick and easy bed. They are comfortable, raised off the ground and ideal if you haven't got time to build a proper shelter.

DID YOU KNOW?
Snakes like shady places, so make shelters in clear areas, away from piles of rocks or logs.

1. *Tie your hammock between two trees. Make notches in the trees to stop the hammock sliding down.*

2. *String a tarpaulin or poncho above the hammock to make a roof to shield you from rain.*

3. *Hang a **mosquito net** around the hammock so you don't get bitten by mosquitoes in the night.*

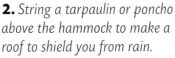

Snow caves and graves

If you're climbing mountains or exploring polar regions, you may get caught in a **blizzard**. It's a frightening experience. Suddenly you're blinded by snow and have no idea what's around you or where you're going. You need to make a shelter, and make it fast.

Dig don't build

There are two types of emergency snow shelters: graves (or trenches) and caves. They both involve digging in the snow rather than building it into walls. This is because digging is easier and quicker than building. Snow caves and graves will keep you warm and protect you from the wind.

*This mountain climber is high on Mount Everest in bad weather. Severe blizzards can cause deadly **whiteouts**.*

DID YOU KNOW?
When making snow shelters, you must stay dry so that your body temperature doesn't fall too low. Keep brushing snow off your clothes before it soaks through.

TRUE SURVIVAL STORY

KEIZO FUNATSU was part of an Antarctic expedition team in 1990. One night he got caught in a blizzard and couldn't find his tent. Keizo quickly dug a trench in the snow and climbed inside to shelter. It was a long, terrifying night. He was so cold that he had to keep getting out and jumping up and down to warm up. Fortunately, he found his tent again in the morning.

Cosy caves

Snow caves are best made in the mountains, where wind blows large banks of snow up against hills and rock faces. This means that it is easy to find a deep pile of snow.

▲ Snow is a great insulator, so a good snow cave will keep you warm.

1. Dig a hole into a deep snow bank with an **ice axe** or snow shovel. If you don't have these tools, try using a **snowshoe**. Make just enough room for you and your equipment.

2. Make air holes with an axe handle, pole or stick. Find something to close the entrance, such as your rucksack or blocks of snow.

Cold air sinks, so make a raised bed of snow to sleep on. Lie on your rucksack or spare clothes so you're not touching the snow.

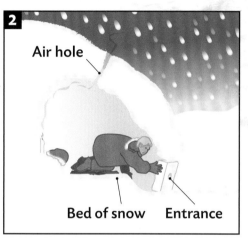

Air hole

Bed of snow   Entrance

Digging trenches

Snow graves are very simple, covered trenches. They are ideal in flat, exposed places such as the Arctic.

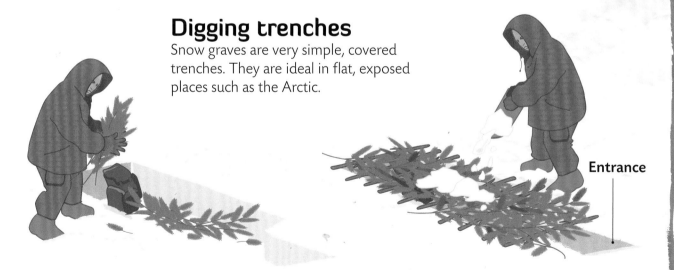

Entrance

1. Dig a trench into the snow. Make sure it's long enough to lie in. Use spare clothes or vegetation such as pine needles to make a warm nest inside.

2. Lay branches over the top and cover them with vegetation or snow. If you can't find branches, pack snow into slabs and lean them against each other.

Making an igloo

Well-built igloos are comfortable, sturdy shelters that can last a long time. However, they take time to build. You also need a **snow saw** or a long knife – and it's useful to have a few friends to help, too!

▲ *A camping guide constructs an igloo in British Columbia, Canada. Once he has all the ice blocks in place, he will fill the gaps with snow.*

TRUE SURVIVAL STORY

VICTOR CAMPBELL was the leader of a six-man Antarctic expedition in 1912. They became cut off from their ship by ice and had to spend the winter in the snow. They dug a cave into a deep snowdrift, then lined the walls with snow blocks to make it stronger. They made the shelter small to preserve heat, but this meant that it was extremely cramped. When a ship finally arrived, seven months later, the men had 'igloo back' from bending over all the time.

Build your own igloo

You need to use hard, compacted snow to make an igloo. If the snow around you seems too soft, stamp on it to pack it down and then leave it to re-freeze.

1. *Mark out a circle on a flat area of snow. Cut out large blocks of snow from inside the circle.*

2. *Position a circle of blocks around the hole. Make sure they lean slightly inwards. Cut away the tops of the first few blocks to make a slope.*

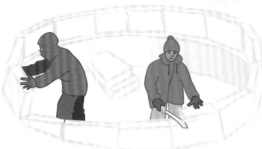

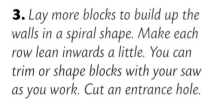

3. *Lay more blocks to build up the walls in a spiral shape. Make each row lean inwards a little. You can trim or shape blocks with your saw as you work. Cut an entrance hole.*

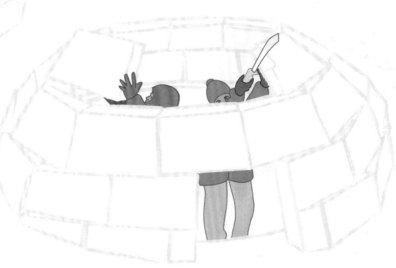

4. *To fill the gap in the top of the dome, place a block on top that is bigger than the hole. Then go inside and trim it to fit in place.*

5. *Smooth the walls inside, then cover the outside with loose snow to fill the cracks. This will freeze overnight and make the igloo stronger.*

6. *Make several air holes in the igloo. Build a raised bed of snow to sleep on and line it with warm blankets or clothes.*

Tunnel built over entrance

Air holes

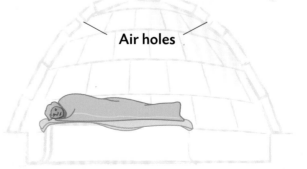

Desert shelters

Camping in the desert is difficult and dangerous. During the day, the sun is fiercely hot. At night, the sky is clear and the temperature plummets. Strong winds whip up blinding sandstorms and sudden rain causes **flash floods**. Shelter is vital – but there are hardly any materials to build with.

▼ *This is Death Valley in California, USA. The best place to shelter might be in cooler hollows between the sand dunes.*

DID YOU KNOW?
Berbers *in Africa use dead camels as emergency desert shelters. They skin and gut the camel, then crawl into the carcass with the skin as a blanket.*

Using a tarpaulin

In the desert, it's very useful to take a tarpaulin and some cord or rope. You can make all kinds of shelters with a tarpaulin. These can be used in any wild place, not just deserts.

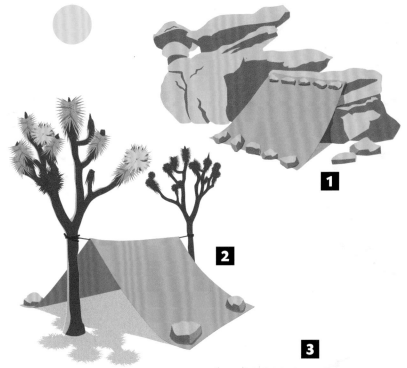

1. *Find a rocky outcrop and make a lean-to. Fix the tarpaulin in place with rocks at the top and bottom.*

2. *If you have some rope or cord, try making a tent instead. String the tarpaulin between two trees. Weigh down the ends with rocks.*

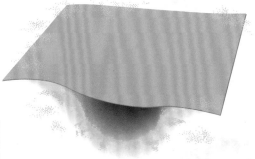

3. *If all else fails, dig a trench in the sand to lie in, then pull the tarpaulin over you. Leave a gap for ventilation. You'll be hot and uncomfortable, but it's better than sitting directly in the sun.*

Keep cool!

Be very careful if you're building a desert shelter during the day. Heat and lack of water will soon make you feel **dehydrated**. Try to rest in the shade and do any physical activity in the evening or even at night. Look for caves or trees that provide shade.

◀ *Desert animals, like this fox, take shelter in the day and come out at night, when it's cooler.*

Prairie homes

Building a shelter can be tricky if you're out on wide, grassy plains such as North American **prairies** or African **savannahs**. The land is flat and there are lots of small shrubs and bushes, but not many trees. The best plan is to carry your own tent or shelter-making materials.

Portable homes

Many nomadic people travel across plains. Nomads called Mongols live in traditional tents called yurts that they take apart and carry from place to place on camels or yaks. Yurts have a circular, wooden frame, which is covered with thick **felt** made from sheep's wool.

▲ *These nomads in Kyrgyzstan are putting up a yurt. A canvas cover is usually added on top of the felt.*

Tipi tents

Tipis (sometimes spelled tepees) are the traditional homes of Native Americans from the **Great Plains**. They are cone-shaped tents of wooden poles, covered with animal skin, bark or canvas. They are the perfect moveable home as they are very quick to take apart and rebuild.

◀ *These tipis were put up in Nebraska, USA, to show how Native Americans used to live.*

DID YOU KNOW?
Soldiers who parachute into unknown territory are taught how to build tipis, using their parachutes as covers.

Make a tarp tipi

You can make your own simple tipi, as long as you have some long poles or sticks, rope and a tarpaulin or waterproof sheet.

1. *Tie three poles together at one end, then stand them up to make a tripod.*

2. *If you have more poles, lean them against the tripod for extra support.*

3. *Wrap tarpaulin around the poles and tie it at the top. Weigh it down with rocks.*

1
2
3

Domed wigwams

Wigwams are also traditional Native American homes, but they aren't the same as tipis. They are strong, domed structures that are usually permanent homes, not portable shelters. They are made with a frame of arched poles and covered with materials such as grass, bark, reeds or cloth.

▲ *Large wigwams have spacious living areas inside. This wigwam even has room for a fire for cooking and keeping warm.*

Stone, turf and log huts

For thousands of years, people have built strong, long-lasting homes using natural materials such as rocks, turf and logs. If you have plenty of time, why not try building one yourself?

Stone homes

In the past, shepherds in hilly or mountainous places made shelters with stone walls and turf roofs. These shelters had to be well-built, as shepherds lived there for months while their animals grazed on the hills.

▼ *These stone and turf huts in the Andes Mountains, Bolivia, were built by local shepherds and farmers.*

TRUE SURVIVAL STORY

FRIDTJOF NANSEN was a Norwegian explorer and scientist. In 1893, he took a crew of 12 men on a daring expedition across the Arctic Ocean in a boat designed to be carried along by drifting ice. The voyage became very difficult during the winter, so they stopped at a tiny island. Fridtjof and his crew built a small hut on the island, using stones for walls and walrus skins for a roof. They managed to live in this stone shelter for nine months before setting off on their journey again.

Making a stone shelter

Building a stone wall looks easy, but it takes a lot of practice. You must be very careful that the wall doesn't collapse on you. Choose large, flat stones that rest firmly on each other.

__1.__ Find a hollow in the ground and build a low wall of stones around it. Fill the gaps with mud and leaves.

__2.__ Make a roof with long branches. If you have a knife, cut squares of turf and lay them on top. This keeps rain out and warmth in.

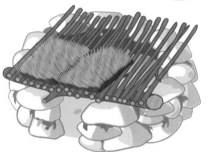

Houses of grass

In countries such as Iceland, where there aren't many trees, turf can be used to build whole houses. First, turf is sliced from the ground, then cut into squares with a tool called a **rutter**. The squares are laid like bricks to make walls or a dome shape. Turf homes keep heat in well and last a long time.

Log cabins

A log cabin is a sturdy, warm forest shelter. Notches are made in the ends of the logs so that they slot together neatly, then the gaps between them are filled with mud and straw. Log cabins take time and skill to build.

These log cabins are in the Yukon, Canada. The cabin on the left is a food store, so it is raised to keep animals out.

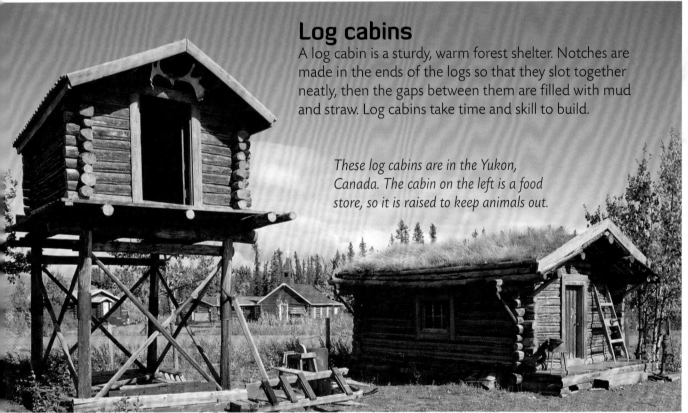

Taking a tent

When you go on a planned expedition in the wilderness, it makes sense to carry a tent. Think carefully about the type of tent you take. Is it big enough for the number of people who need to sleep in it? Is it suitable for the climate and weather? Can you carry it and do you know how to put it up?

▼ *These hikers in Scotland have packed all their camping equipment in rucksacks.*

TRUE SURVIVAL STORY

STEVE THIBEAULT is a keen hiker who once took his children camping in woods in North Carolina, USA. When they stopped to put up their tent, Steve realized that he'd forgotten to bring tent poles. Instead of panicking, he strung rope between two trees, hung the tent over it and weighed down the ends. His shelter kept them safe all night.

Choosing a shape

The most basic tents are ridge tents, which have an 'A'-shaped frame at the front and back with a long pole between them. Ridge tents are strong, but the sloping sides mean there isn't much room inside. Tunnel tents have more space, and are quick to put up, but their shape makes them less stable. Dome tents are strong and spacious, but they are heavy to carry.

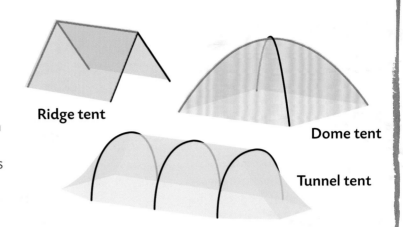

Ridge tent

Dome tent

Tunnel tent

The toughest tent

If you're camping in the mountains or expecting bad weather, use a geodesic tent. These tents have a **streamlined** dome shape and are built with criss-crossing poles, which makes them very stable in high winds. There is also plenty of space inside. However, they can be complicated to put up, so make sure you practise at home first!

◀ *This climber is using a geodesic tent in the Rhone Alps, France.*

Tent tips

Choose a clear, flat place to pitch your tent, with the entrance away from the wind. Dig a small drainage trench around it so rain water can run away. Always use pegs or rocks to weigh down your tent, and take a repair kit to fix any tears or holes.

Dry and warm

Most tents have an extra layer, called a fly sheet, which helps to keep them dry. In very cold places, you could try adding extra insulation by covering your tent with branches and a layer of snow. Even better, build an igloo – it may well be warmer than a tent!

◀ *Snow is very heavy, so make a frame of branches rather than piling it directly on to your tent.*

Test your survival skills

Are you ready to build your own shelters in the wild? Take this quiz and discover whether you've learned the bushcraft skills you'll need to survive. You can find the answers on page 32.

1. What's the one thing every emergency shelter MUST have?
a) Soft vegetation to lie on.
b) Space to stretch out in.
c) A domed shape.
d) Air holes for ventilation.

2. What's the name of the hut below?
a) Yurt   b) Wigwam   c) Aqal   d) Tipi

3. What is a geodesic tent?
a) A tent with an 'A'-shaped frame.
b) A tent with criss-crossing poles.
c) A tent that fits in your pocket.
d) A tent covered in layers of felt and canvas.

4. Which of these sentences about domed-shaped shelters is false?
a) They can create a big, airy room.
b) They allow rain to drain off easily.
c) They are only used in snowy places.
d) They can withstand strong winds.

5. Where's the best place to build a shelter in this forest?

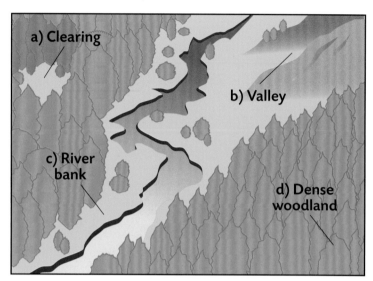
a) Clearing
b) Valley
c) River bank
d) Dense woodland

6. You're stranded on a mountain. Night is falling and it's snowing hard. What kind of shelter should you make?
a) Snow grave
b) Snow cave
c) Igloo
d) Lean-to

7. You're building a shelter in the jungle. Which of these designs is the best?

a)

b)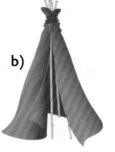

c)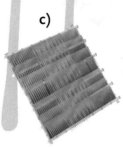

d)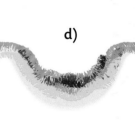

8. What kind of snow do you need to build an igloo?
a) Soft and powdery.
b) Heavy and wet.
c) Hard and compacted.
d) Any kind.

9. You're lost in the desert in the heat of the midday sun. You come to some trees. What should you do?
a) Pull off branches and make a lean-to.
b) Don't go near them – wild animals could be lurking there.
c) Rest in the shade of the trees until evening.
d) Keep going, but come back at night to sleep there.

10. What is a howff?
a) A type of cave.
b) A tool for sawing ice blocks.
c) A lightweight emergency tent.
d) A stone and turf hut.

11. Why are the shelters in this photograph built on stilts?
a) To stay warm.
b) To avoid floods.
c) To give people a good view.
d) To keep out mosquitoes.

12. When might you need to use a tool called a rutter?
a) Cutting turf.
b) Slicing palm leaves.
c) Shovelling snow.
d) Putting up a hammock.

Glossary

avalanche   A large slide of snow, ice or rocks down a mountain.

Berber   A member of a group of people from North Africa. Many Berber people live in nomadic tribes.

blizzard   A severe winter storm that consists of low temperatures, strong winds and very heavy, blowing snow.

bushcraft   Skills and knowledge that you need to survive in the wilderness.

carbon dioxide   A gas in the air around us. You make carbon dioxide in your body as a waste product, and get rid of it when you breathe out. In small, unventilated areas, the level of carbon dioxide can build up until it is dangerously high. Inhaling too much carbon dioxide makes you drowsy and dizzy, and could eventually make you lose consciousness.

crevasse   A deep crack in an ice sheet or a glacier, which is a large mass of ice.

dehydrated   Suffering from loss of water from your body. It is dangerous to become too dehydrated because your body cannot work properly without water. Take regular sips of water to avoid becoming dehydrated.

felt   A type of fabric that is made by pressing together strands of wool, fur or hair, instead of weaving them. Felt can be a very thick, tough material.

flash flood   A sudden flood that is caused by short-lived but very heavy rain.

frostbite   A painful medical condition in which skin and other tissue in the human body is damaged because of extreme cold.

Great Plains   The large region of open, grassy land, or prairie, that covers the central part of the USA and spreads up into Canada and down into Mexico.

hammock   A wide strip of canvas or net that is hung above the ground, usually between two trees, and used as a bed.

howff   A stone cave that is formed naturally when one large, flat rock lies on top of smaller rocks. Howffs are found in mountainous areas of Scotland.

ice axe   A mountaineering tool with a head that is pointed at one end and flat at the other. The flat end is for hacking steps or footholds in snow and ice, while the pointed end is used to get a grip in the snow and stop you slipping.

igloo   A dome-shaped shelter built with blocks of solid snow. The word igloo means 'house' in the Inuit language. The Inuit people are from Arctic regions in Canada, Greenland and Alaska.

insulation   Materials that are used to prevent heat escaping as it rises.

landslide   The sliding of a large amount of rocks or soil down the side of a mountain or cliff.

mosquito net   A fine, see-through mesh curtain or sheet that lets air in, but keeps flies, mosquitoes and other insects out. Mosquitoes can carry diseases such as malaria.

nomadic Living as a nomad. Nomads are members of tribes or groups who move from place to place with herds of animals. Nomadic people are skilled at putting up temporary shelters that they can dismantle when they set off again.

poncho A large sheet of waterproof fabric with holes for your head and arms to fit through. A poncho can be useful as a raincoat and also as material to make a simple shelter.

prairie A treeless, grassy plain. Prairies are found in central areas of the USA and Canada.

rutter A small, flat, sharp-edged spade used for cutting turf into blocks.

savannah Open grassy land, usually with scattered bushes or trees. There are lots of savannahs in tropical Africa.

snow saw A long, thin knife with a sharp, jagged edge that is specially designed to cut easily through blocks of snow.

snowshoe A wide, flat base that attaches under your shoe to help you walk across snow.

streamlined Smooth and curved, so wind blows over and around easily, without getting blocked by awkwardly-shaped parts.

tarpaulin A heavy sheet made of canvas or a similar material and coated with tar, wax or paint to make it waterproof. Tarpaulins usually have small holes around the edges for attaching rope.

thatched Covered with straw, reeds, rushes or grasses to make a thick, watertight roof.

turf The top layer of grassy ground that consists of grass, matted roots and soil.

ventilation A good flow of air through holes or gaps in a roof or other solid structure. This lets fresh air in and waste gases out.

whiteout A condition caused when a blizzard, thick clouds and snow on the ground make everything a confusing blur of white.

Useful websites

www.bushcraftliving.com
Learn about all kinds of bushcraft and survival skills, including making shelters.

www.ravenlore.co.uk
Discover lots of useful tips and ideas for living in the wilderness.

www.outdoor-survival-guide.com/survival/ survival_skills/survival_shelter
Read about all kinds of shelters in the wild.

www.wildwoodsurvival.com/survival/shelter/ index.html
Follow links to great shelter facts and photos.

Index

Answers to survival skills quiz (pages 28-29)

1d, 2c, 3b, 4c, 5a, 6b, 7a, 8c, 9c, 10a, 11b, 12a